THE DUNNY SEAT

The Dunny Seat was expertly crafted from the finest materials sourced from certain numbered aisles from a well known hardware store in Australia.

DO NOT
ENTER

From the Author

Aussies love the bush, even if we've never been there. Vast expanses of nothing highlighted with rugged beauty and awesome splendor. It's who we are.

These days, most who venture into this Mad Max wilderness do so in mobile homes, caravans and glamper trailers and miss one of its sheer pleasures – the Dunny View.

While 24hr stopovers and toilet cubicles provide a convenient location for our daily movements, the Dunny View offers so much more. It presents to you the authenticity of nature and reassures you of your small, but significant, part in it. It lays bare the truth and glory of our vulnerability and calls us to embrace it.

This collection of Dunny Views comes from the Western Australian outback – a region extending from the northern inland Pilbara, through the Gascoyne and Murchison, to the Southern Goldfields east of Norseman.

So, next time you're travelling through this great land and you're feeling the morning call, grab your shovel and dunny roll and wander twenty or thirty paces into the bush to experience one of life's simple pleasures – the Dunny View.

Regards,
Jamie Nunn.

MAP OF WESTERN AUSTRALIA

In these dunny views, "The Outback" is depicted by the Pilbara, Mid-West (Gascoyne/ Murchison) and Goldfields. Other regions like the Kimberley and Interior, have their own, distinctive beauty.

1. North of Tom Price
2. The "Orange" Red Centre
3. A Prospector's Camp – Hillside Station
4. The Burning Bush
5. Meekatharra Roadhouse
6. Clear Skies
7. Skull Springs
8. Seeds
9. The Ironclad Hotel – Marble Bar
10. Mulga Downs Station
11. Morning Moon
12. Eyes in the Dark
13. Out in the Open
14. Remote
15. Mount Augustus
16. The De Grey River
17. Termite Mound
18. 24-Hour Stopover
19. 43º Waterhole
20. Animal Tracks
21. 29 Days
22. Emu Rock – Ex Credo Station
23. Broad Arrow
24. Road to Nowhere
25. Ashburton Downs
26. The Goldfields
27. Cow Dung
28. Southern Cross
29. Clean Wind
30. Creeks
31. Sunrise near Roy Hill
32. Sunrise at Minnie Creek
33. The Outback

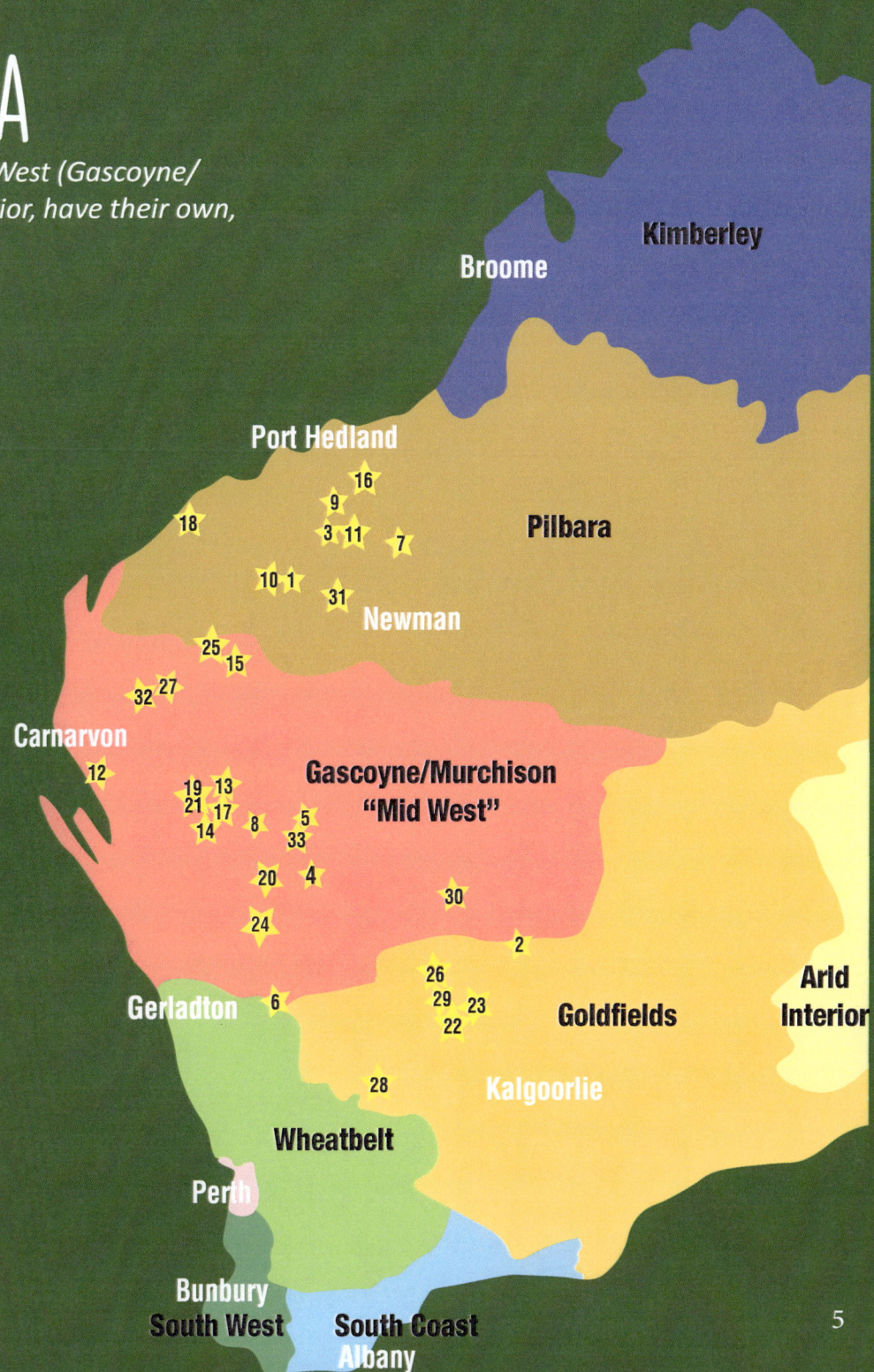

Kimberley

Broome

Port Hedland

Pilbara

Newman

Carnarvon

Gascoyne/Murchison "Mid West"

Geraldton

Goldfields

Arid Interior

Kalgoorlie

Wheatbelt

Perth

Bunbury
South West

South Coast
Albany

INTRODUCTION

After spending much time in the remote parts of Western Australia – usually with few modern conveniences – it became apparent that the views one had when taking the first ablutions of the day were often the best views one could have anywhere in the world. They were interesting, stimulating and sometimes just plain boring, but due to their perspective, they were different from the views one would usually stop to see.

Unlike the awe-inspiring photographs of majestic places that you will find in a professional photographer's collection, the pictures in this book are simple. They were taken on a Samsung Galaxy S5 phone while sitting on the Dunny Seat in the quiet and cool of the morning. The camera was set on auto. The light was not adjusted, the colors were not enhanced and little thought was put into the angle of the shot. However, the author did get daring and sometimes used the panoramic setting.

Each picture has a story – a comment or anecdote that adds context. Like the pictures, the stories are simple. Some are funny, some are ponderous, some are both. Within these, you will find your own gems. You will be taken to forgotten times and places from your own life that have made you laugh and wonder.

Child-like in their simplicity, these dunny views are more than just nice photos. They are reminders that when we remove the walls we build and take time to sit, we become aware of the depth and beauty of our surroundings. Whether in the Outback or the 'burbs, we can rejoice that we are a significant part of something bigger than ourselves.

THE VIEWS

NORTH OF TOM PRICE

I chucked out half a lettuce here. It had been up against the cooling element of my car fridge and was frost burnt. Nothing worse than soggy lettuce (although it is good tadpole food, if ever you get pet tadpoles).

After I had tossed it out, I looked at it sitting under a young, bushy tree like the one in this photo. It looked out of place. Lettuces are not supposed to be nestling under trees in the Pilbara. So I thought, "Am I littering?"

My personal definition of littering is discarding something in a place that it is not supposed to be, unless it is buried. I created that definition because I don't like turning up to campsites with tea bags and orange peel dropped onto old campfires. By that definition, I was littering.

So I left it there and started to work on a new definition that doesn't include lettuce but does include orange peel.

THE "ORANGE" RED CENTRE

The desert here is vast and flat. All the vegetation is grey. Alive or dead, it's grey. But the dirt is orange.

This is our Red Centre.

I think the people that first referred to "Australia's Red Centre" only said that because it sounds better than "Australia's Orange Centre," which sounds more like a large citrus processing factory.

A PROSPECTOR'S CAMP — HILLSIDE STATION

Sometimes, when you head off the main track looking for a waterhole, there's already someone there. This one was occupied by a prospector who spends ten or twelve weeks here alone, every year, searching for his precious. As most do in the bush, he welcomed me openly and told me of the many exploits of his younger days.

His dunny, on which I am sitting, was a blue, plastic 44 gallon drum with a hole cut in the top and a white plastic toilet seat screwed on. The hole underneath fell deeply into the earth. No gold nuggets down there....

THE BURNING BUSH

God appeared to Moses in a burning bush. He had been wandering around the outback in the middle east at the time (Moses, that is, not God).

I sat by this bush for longer than was necessary, wondering if it would suddenly burst into flame. No, not wondering – urging it to. I wanted to see it burst into flame and have God speak to me.

It didn't.

Then I wondered, if I had enough faith, would it have burst into flames then?

MEEKATHARRA ROADHOUSE

Sometimes you are lucky enough to come across a roadhouse that has free shower facilities as well as a dunny. Meekatharra Roadhouse is one of those. After a few days in the bush, a date with a flush toilet followed by a nice warm shower brings back a true appreciation of life's simple pleasures. Even this view has a bit to offer, like, "I wonder where the soap dispenser is now?"

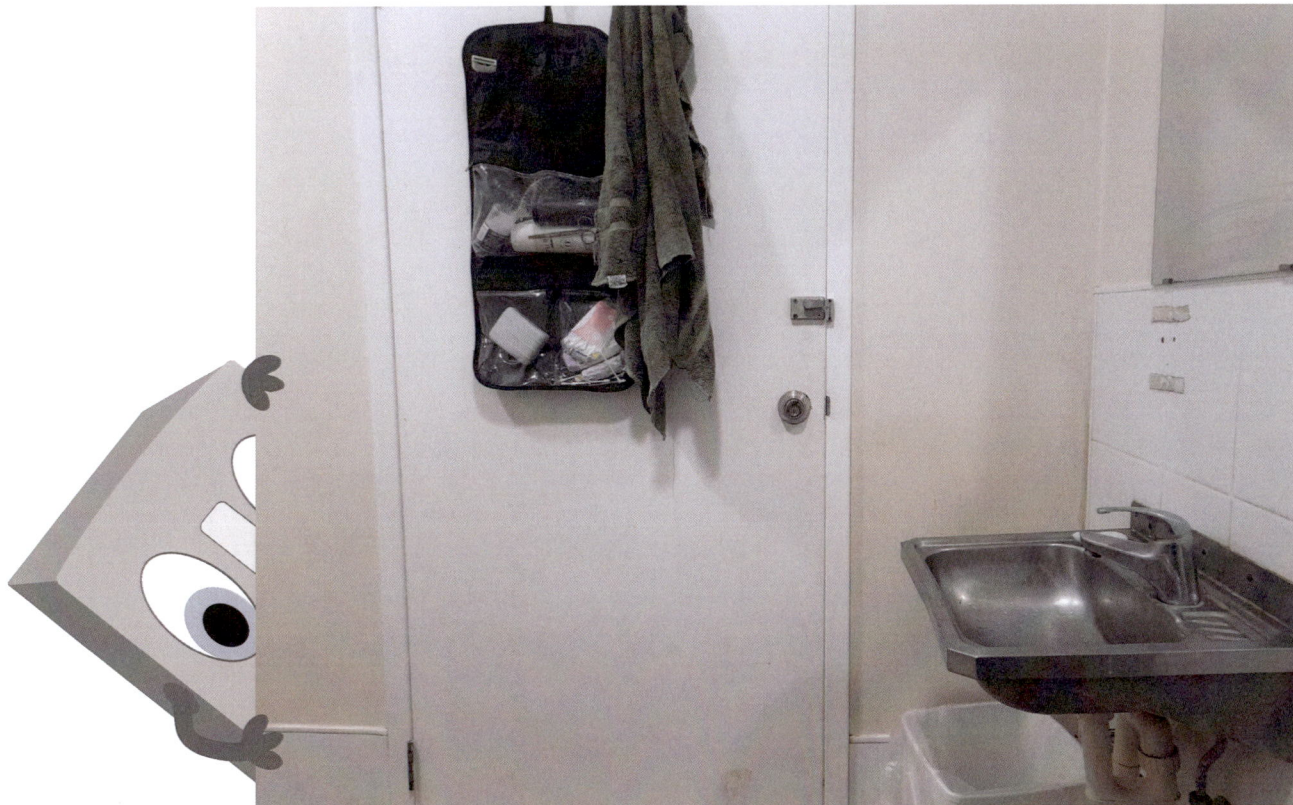

CLEAR SKIES

Heading north after months in suburbia, the first morning in the bush is when it starts to sink in. The first clear sky. The first smell of open air and arid earth. The first sound of silence.

Waking up here, with nothing and no-one around, gives stark clarity that I am in charge of myself.

There is an adventure to be had.

How I do it is completely up to me.

SKULL SPRINGS

A fair trot east of Nullagine, off a quiet track that lulls you into thinking it's in reasonable condition until you travel round a sweeping bend over a blind crest onto a steep slope that turns into a rollercoaster of loose rocks and washouts, sits Skull Springs.

After a moment of sheer terror, you curse the heat and the dust and the lack of signage, wondering why the hell you left your clean, air-conditioned house in the city.

But, a short while later, you come across this beautiful oasis. Cooling off in the clear, fresh water, washing away dust and heat, watching little fish explore your arms and legs while listening to the quiet sounds in the trees as the sun sets below a pink, orange and purple sky, life becomes timeless. The perfect antidote for cars and roads.

SEEDS

Acacia tetragonaphylla, known as "Curara", is a prickly bugger with needley leaves that come to a sharp point at the end. The seeds themselves are very pretty. This one is full of pods containing black seeds surrounded by an orange aril.

I've been told that witchetty grubs chew their way along the roots and that you can find them by listening for a hollow sound when you tap the ground around the base of the tree.

I don't know if my teachers were being honest, or if they wanted to see this white fella make a fool of himself crawling around with his ear to the ground under a prickly tree!

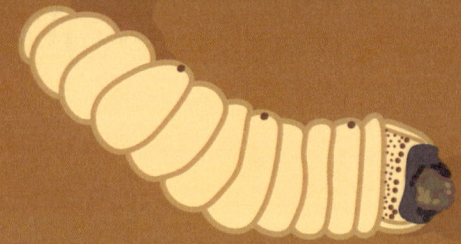

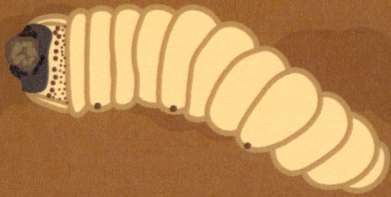

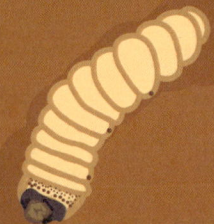

THE IRONCLAD HOTEL — MARBLE BAR

A mainstay of my seed collecting trips, the Ironclad Hotel houses proof that the stories and characters of the Australian bush are not myths. There you will find the ancient prospector, the truck driver, the pool shark and the larrikin. You'll be served by a barmaid who will give you a smile and a chat (and send you out on your ear if you try any funny business) and you'll see station owners whose endless toil lives in the crevices of their faces and hands. And, if you take your time, if you watch but don't stare, if you listen before thinking and think before speaking, and talk in quiet tones, you will also find the deep wisdom contained within the spirit of our First People.

MULGA DOWNS STATION

Mulga Downs is a bit north-east of Tom Price in the Pilbara. It was the home of billionaire Lang Hancock (before he was a billionaire). From here he started Western Australia's iron ore industry and, more infamously, the mining of asbestos at a town called Wittenoom.

MORNING MOON

Stepping through spinifex, cattle wander costively through the landscape, bovine beasts on an endless trek to nowhere. The moon watches and goes to bed before the stones start to cry out against the heat.

NOTE: There are no cattle in this picture. They left during the night. I could've taken a photo with cattle in it the previous afternoon and passed it off as a morning dunny view, but the moon wouldn't be there, the sun would, and the shadows would be pointing in the wrong direction and it wouldn't be a morning moon dunny view, but an afternoon photo of cows and the sun.

EYES IN THE DARK

At about 9.00pm, after a couple of coldies in Carnarvon, I pulled up off a small track and climbed into my swag. The night was pitch black. As I zipped up, my head torch shone into some bushes where I saw two glowing eyes peering back at me.

Slowly, quietly, I got out of my swag and grabbed the dunny shovel. I crept around the bushes. The eyes followed me, then disappeared. Clenching the shovel, I worked my way around. Was it an injured fox? A goat? Please don't be... In the back of my mind I knew it was an evil, demon death hound craving the flesh of lone campers. I glanced behind me, like they never do in the movies, to make sure they weren't working in packs. Creeping around the back, slowly, I built up the nerve to get closer. Then, BAM! I found a pile of old beer bottles reflecting the light from my torch. I felt a bit dumb.

Climbing back into my swag, it took me a while to get to sleep. I kept the shovel close by.

The next morning I set up the dunny seat to ponder the bottles. I thought about the blokes, and maybe women, who had drank them and stacked them here. Were they building the fence behind me? Or was it a mustering camp? Or maybe they had to offload all the empties on their way home from a fishing trip so they didn't get in trouble with the missus.

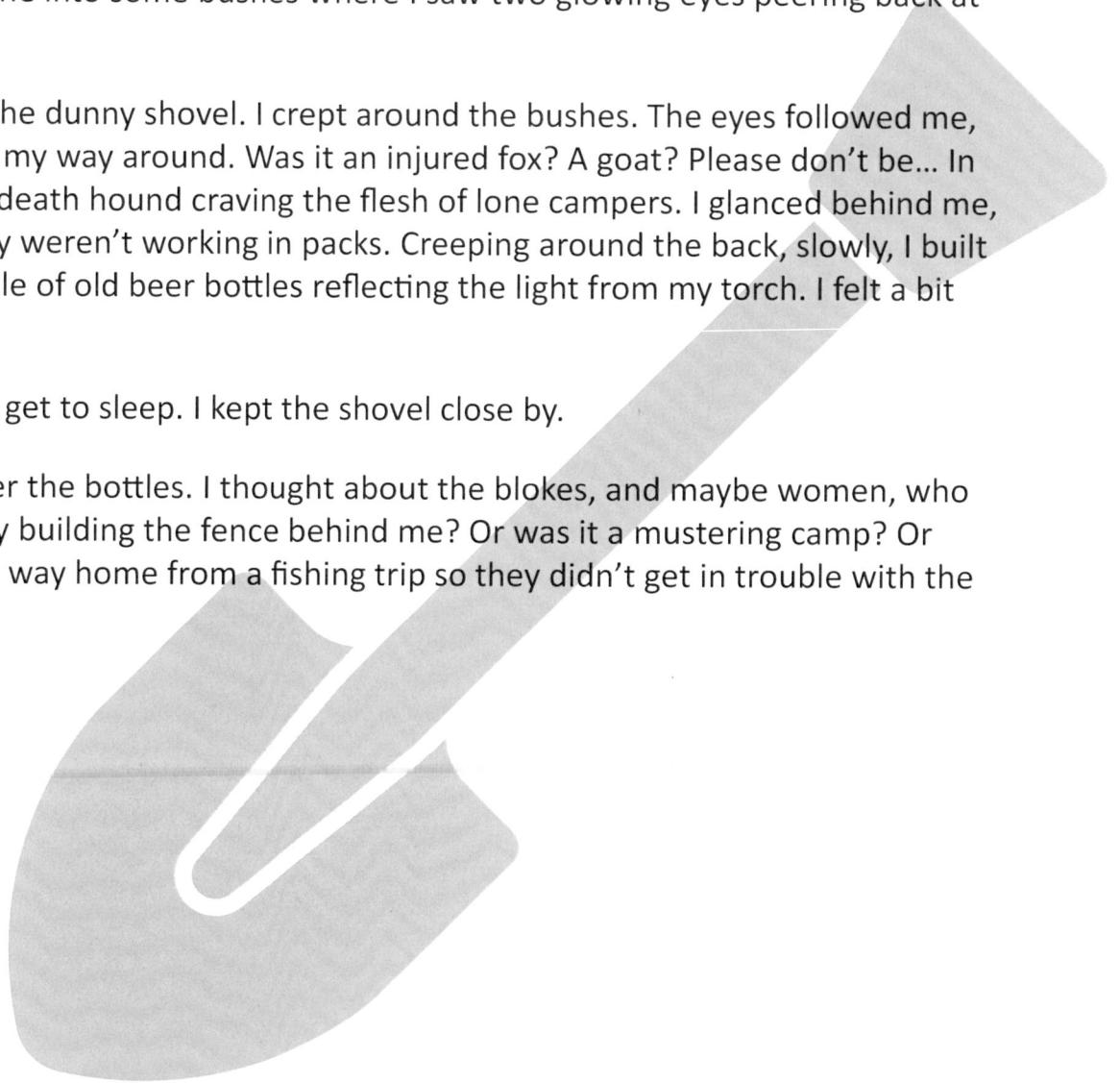

OUT IN THE OPEN

On the Dunny Seat, sometimes there's just nowhere to hide. It's a good thing not many people drive past here at this time of the morning, or afternoon, or evening...

REMOTE

The Mid-West region of Western Australia is remote. Apart from the deserts of the Interior, it is the most remote part of Australia. Some people will laugh when I say this, but it is true. It is more remote than outback Queensland, New South Wales, the Kimberly or the Pilbara.

For example, if you take the widest part of Far North Queensland, say, Townsville to Normanton, you will travel 840 kilometres on bitumen road and pass through half a dozen towns with populations around 200 along the way. The same is true of Southern Queensland and Western New South Wales.
In the Mid-West, on the other hand, you can run out of fuel travelling the main road from Wiluna to Carnarvon. It's 804km, all dirt, and there are only two towns in between. One lonely stretch is 448km long. It's the same in other directions too.

There may be other places that are more rugged, drier, wetter or harder to access, but as for emptiness, the Mid-West is the emptiest.

MOUNT AUGUSTUS

This is not Mount Augustus, it is a little hill. But it is near Mount Augustus.

I set up camp here next to a line of trees to protect me from the south easterlies. After my morning toilet, I wandered over to the hill to have a look. Maybe a big gold nugget had exposed itself and was waiting for me. If it did, I couldn't find it. Instead there was a track worn by kangaroos semi-circling the base. I wondered what the view from the top would be like.

I still don't know. I didn't climb it. I think I was hungry, or maybe I remembered that my cup of tea was going cold.

33

THE DE GREY RIVER

This is one of the most welcome places in the Pilbara; a truly wonderful oasis in the open.
After many days collecting native seed in the hot, scratchy, dusty bush, your thoughts
immediately turn from, "What the hell am I doing out here?" to
"This has to be the most wonderful place on earth!"

TERMITE MOUND

There's nothing particularly interesting about this one, but whenever I see them I wonder where all the termites have gone. I have never found one with termites in it and have long stopped chopping them up to see.

24 HOUR STOPOVER

This is the view inside a 24 hour stop-over toilet cubicle.

Even the camera doesn't like it.

43° WATERHOLE

I came to the Mid-West from down south and was collecting native seed for mine site revegetation. As the day warmed up, around 8.30am, I started feeling hotter and hotter. I stopped every 20 minutes or so only to collapse onto my folder chair, guzzle a litre of water and pour the rest over my head. I thought I was getting soft. A warm day in the Murchison and this weak southerner can't handle it! I was buggered if I was gonna be soft, so I kept going until the patch was done. It was 1.30pm.

Completely knackered, I figured the coolest place to be was in the car with the air-conditioner on. So I started the car and read the thermometer – 43°C! I wasn't getting soft after all – even the air-conditioner struggled! I went for a drive to find more seed but didn't care if I found any or not – at least I was cool!
I followed the GPS around a cobweb of non-tracks for an hour and a half before stumbling across this waterhole. It was only 5k's from where I had been picking. I stripped to my undies (no further, because these waterholes often contain rather bold and rather large yabbies) and plunged chest deep into the cool water. I floated around for an hour.

Just a stone's throw away, a flotilla of ducks were countering my actions. When I moved towards them, they moved away. When I stopped, they stopped. I pretended, for a short time, to be a crocodile.

When I extracted myself from the water it took about 3 minutes to feel as hot as I did before. I wanted to go straight back in but I had a heap of gear back at my seed collecting spot. So I went back, packed up, and moved back here.

It was 5.30pm when I returned. I checked the thermometer – 39 degrees. This photo is the view from my dunny seat the next morning.

ANIMAL TRACKS

Most creeks in the outback have sandy bottoms that get written on by animals. Lizards, kangaroos, snakes and birds leave impressions of their feet, tails and bellies, impressions that tell of wandering and hunting: an upright stance, a twitching ear, a startled take-off.

I try to figure out which way the creek flows and which direction the snake was going and I wonder if, maybe someday, I could spend a year or two with an old Aboriginal man who could teach me these things.

29 DAYS

One thing you notice when camping in the bush is the changing phase of the moon. It takes 29 days for a full cycle. Sometimes the nights are pitch black. Other times the nights are so well lit that it's difficult to sleep.

A full moon is magnificent; a new moon reveals the brilliance of the stars.

EMU ROCK — EX CREDO STATION

This unassumingly impressive place envelopes one in the age and vastness of Australia. Unfortunately, this photo doesn't show it very well. What is does show is me sitting on the dunny seat.

If you ever go there, a brief walk up and over this rock will reveal the impressiveness that I am talking about.

BROAD ARROW

Air conditioning is a great thing. So are a good night's sleep on a comfortable bed and a bit of cricket on the telly. Sometimes the dunny view has to be sacrificed for this.

ROAD TO NOWHERE

It's not a track. It's a bare strip that runs through the bush. It doesn't go anywhere. It doesn't really even start anywhere.

I have followed a few of these non-tracks. Most only go for a few hundred meters, and when they end I always feel like a bit of a dill as I try to reverse my trailer out of the deadend, vowing never to follow one again. But they always look so enticing!

ASHBURTON DOWNS

The land around Ashburton Downs feels coarse and uncaring. I don't like it.

In the outback it is not uncommon to feel the spirit of the places you travel through. Ask our first people, the custodians, they'll tell you. Some places feel kind and peaceful and some have a spirit of joy. Others are serious and warn you. Most are truly wonderful. But to me, the country around Ashburton feels abrasive.

I have travelled through land where I sense nothing but evil; fearful, dark, angry places that reach into your soul and expose your most base and inexorable fears. Ashburton Downs is not like that. Instead, this land evokes desolation. It is feels empty; bereft. It feels like that which remains when we use our land as a place to own rather than a place to love.

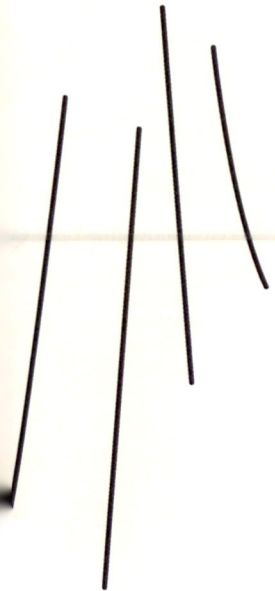

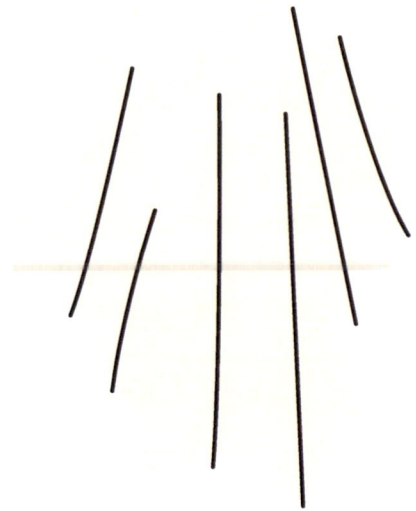

THE GOLDFIELDS

There is gold here. Lots of gold.

Scratch the surface. Scrape away the rocks and tufts and bushes and trees. Drill a hole. Dig a big hole. Dig out the loam and clay and rocks and cart it away in big trucks and crush it and wash it in huge vats.

Electrify the liquid and scrape off the gold and pump off the thick, left-over soup into dams and piles on the ground to thicken and harden into new hills. Then sprinkle some seed over it, find a new place and do it again.

There is gold here. Lots of gold.

COW DUNG

Not a lot of thought was put into this photo. It could've been one of those mornings when the brain needed a bit of aerostart. Either that, or this was the most interesting thing in this particular spot. I can't say, because I don't remember.

SOUTHERN CROSS

Don't get me wrong, Southern Cross is a great place. My grandfather's legacy lives there and the Railway Hotel has the best pizzas in the world. But for all that, this motel has a perfect example of a dunny view that is simply uninspiring.

CLEAN WIND

There is something nice about windmills. Their clean energy; their rhythmic squeak. Windmills bring water up from the earth and fill tanks from dams. If only we could make our food using clean energy.

CREEKS

The outback bursts into flood. Vast plains catch thundery rains flowing in sheets into creeks like this. The turbulent torrents criss-cross the land, heaving, cascading, into monstrous rivers that run for hundreds of miles. Rivers like the Gascoyne, Lyon and Murchison. Rivers that wipe out towns in a few short hours.

And this is where it starts.

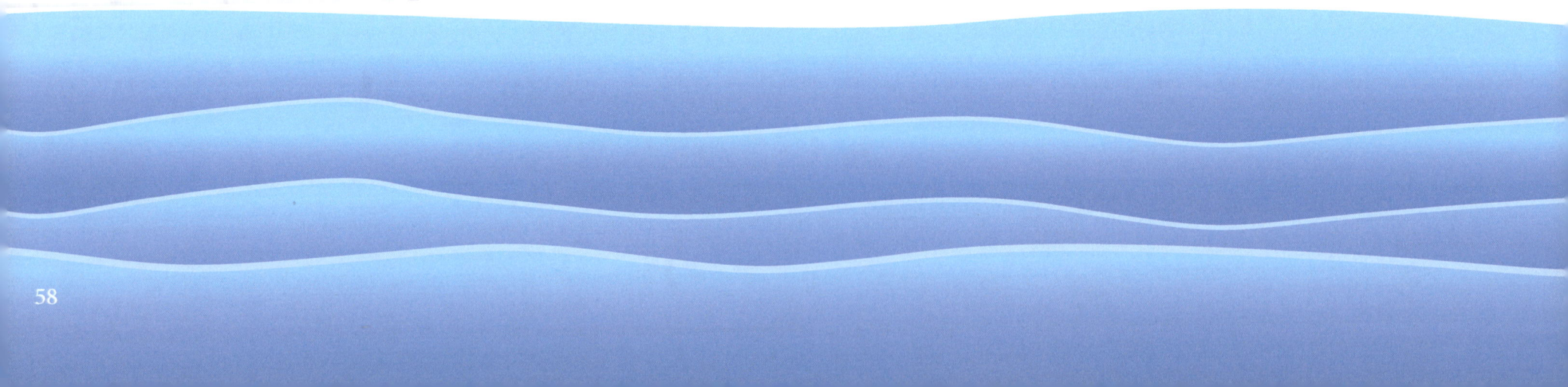

SUNRISE NEAR ROY HILL

Every day the sunrise is different.

SUNRISE AT MINNIE CREEK

THE OUTBACK

The beautiful outback. Lizards live here.

About the Author

Jamie Nunn was born in Perth, Western Australia, in 1970. He spent his early years in Bunbury but moved back to Perth in 1978 and considers himself a "Belmont Boy". After doing worse than he should have in high school, he worked various factory jobs until getting a degree in Biology. He met his wife at Uni and it has been said that he is punching above his weight.

They moved to Mt Barker in 1998 where they had three children. Jamie realised it was time to get a real job, so completed a teaching diploma. He started a career as a Science teacher in Mt Barker in 2002 and has held various positions throughout WA ever since.

Apart from teaching and writing, Jamie travels north every year collecting native seed for land rehabilitation.

www.ingramcontent.com/pod-product-compliance
Lightning Source LLC
Chambersburg PA
CBRC091141030426
42334CB00011B/124